Introduct

The attractive town of Knighto
is well situated in the beautiful Teme vall
Radnorshire and south Shropshire hills. Near tl
Offa's Dyke Path, Knighton is also the starting point for Glyndŵr's Way National Trail. There are two other long distance routes within easy distance of Knighton – the Jack Mytton Way (further along the Teme Valley, in Shropshire) and the Herefordshire Trail, which runs to the east and south-east of the town.

Exploring Knighton itself is a pleasure, making use of quiet streets, lanes and paths to find a mixture of excellent views and attractive old style cottages. A network of footpaths, bridleways, green lanes and other unsurfaced tracks can be found throughout the area, and other local routes pass the Spaceguard Centre (observatory for 'near Earth objects' with an interesting array of telescopes and other astronomical equipment and displays), a number of attractive local pools, oak and mixed woodland and wooded dingles, a large prehistoric hillfort and the impressive Holloway Rocks above nearby Stowe.

The Heart of Wales Railway Line also passes through the town and can be used to access linear walks to and from the adjacent stations at Knucklas, with its impressive 13-arch railway viaduct, and Bucknell, an attractive village of half-timbered and thatched dwellings in the Redlake valley.

Knighton is the base for the Offa's Dyke Association which operates the Offa's Dyke Heritage Centre (01547 528753) within the town. This is the starting point for the circular walking routes that begin within the town and for those that follow a linear route to Knucklas and Bucknell.

Each walk includes a map and directions, enabling the route to be followed easily. The majority of footpaths and bridleways are waymarked by Powys County Council, Shropshire Countryside Services Team and Herefordshire County Council. The long distance routes also have their own distinctive waymarking symbols. Details of Heart of Wales train times can be obtained from the Offa's Dyke Heritage Centre and the station.

The use of walking boots and suitable clothing for walks contained in this guide is recommended. Walkers are also advised to check weather forecasts, particularly if following upland paths (www.metoffice.gov.uk). The location of each walk and its starting point is shown on and inside the back cover, with estimated walking times. Allow extra time if visiting places of interest on the route. Please always follow the country code – and enjoy your walking!.

AROUND KNIGHTON

DESCRIPTION An easy walk of about 3¾ miles with one section of ascent, to the south of Knighton. This walk starts from the Offa's Dyke Heritage Centre and follows an attractive footpath route past plinths commemorating Offa's Dyke Path long distance walking route before following a short section of the River Teme through woods and across a pleasant riverside meadow with views towards Garth Hill. From here, the route loops back into the town, taking a back lane and then path, with further views, to join Glyndŵr's Way and olther lanes for a walk around hidden corners of Knighton. Joining Offa's Dyke Path near the Knighton Hotel, the walk climbs to Frydd Wood and then follows a further lane up towards the Golf Course. Branching off onto a footpath gives additional views down onto Knighton, to which the route now descends to join an attractive riverside lane below Kinsley Wood. After just over half a mile, the route rejoins Offa's Dyke Path for a riverside walk back to Offa's Dyke Heritage Centre. Allow some 2¼ hours for the walk.

START Offa's Dyke Heritage Centre, Knighton SO 285725.

I From outside the Offa's Dyke Heritage Centre, follow the driveway round to the back of the building. Follow the gravel path past two benches and round to the left, to reach a picnic table. Continue ahead for a short distance to reach the first Offa's Dyke Commemorative plinth. Take the path that runs left from the Plinth, descending with wooden railings to the right. At the bottom, turn RIGHT and follow the path to the left of a newly laid hedge to reach the second, large, plinth. Turn RIGHT here and cross Offa's Dyke. Head for the clear path running across the grass and turn LEFT on this to descend towards the River Teme, with further railings to the left. Turn LEFT on the riverside path, passing the site of an old bridge that marks the boundary between Wales and England,

and go thrugh a kissing gate into a riverside meadow. Follow the gravelled path until nearly reaching a second kissing gate. Turn LEFT at this point and head towards the far left corner of the field, following a path that becomes clearer in its latter stages. Go through a kissing gate onto the road.

2 Turn LEFT and follow the road to a T-junction. Turn RIGHT and follow the road up to attractive cottages ahead. Take the turning off to the left, passing further attractive properties, to reach the Plough Inn (on the right). Turn RIGHT just after the Plough Inn, going down Plough Road. At the bottom, bear RIGHT following Glyndŵr's Way on a path down past metal railings. Cross a lane and contine downhill on Glyndŵr's Way path. On reaching a further lane, go RIGHT. Follow the lane and then path past Weaver's Cottage and along to the right of a brook. On reaching the junction with a lane, turn RIGHT and follow this back towards central Knighton. Go past the place where Glyndŵr's Way crosses the lane. After another few yards, take a tarmac path down to the right. On reaching a lane, turn LEFT. Follow the lane along past the Town Crier's House (on the left). After a few yards, turn RIGHT onto a lane that leads to a footbridge. Cross and go LEFT following the path alongside the brook to reach the car park near the Knighton Hotel.

3 Turn SHARP RIGHT and follow Offa's Dyke Path for some 150 yards up Larkey Lane, *passing a bench from which there are good views back towards Knighton.* At the top, cross the main road with care and go RIGHT for a short way. At Offa's Dyke Waymark Post, go LEFT and aim for the gap between the houses (signposted for numbers 31–42). Turn RIGHT just before the garages. After passing the front of the garages, look out for Offa's Dyke Path waymarking on a path leading up to the left. Follow this path up to and across a lane. Go up the steps and continue up through the wood. On reaching a junction in the path, by a small Offa's Dyke Path plinth on the left, turn LEFT and follow a path that gradually descends towards the lane. Turn RIGHT and follow the lane

2

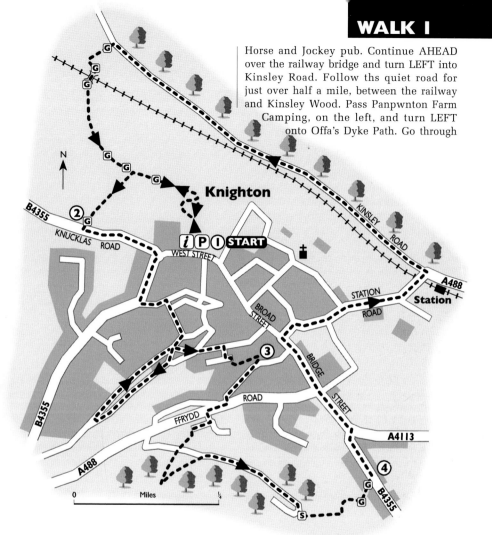

Horse and Jockey pub. Continue AHEAD over the railway bridge and turn LEFT into Kinsley Road. Follow ths quiet road for just over half a mile, between the railway and Kinsley Wood. Pass Panpwnton Farm Camping, on the left, and turn LEFT onto Offa's Dyke Path. Go through

up towards the Golf Club. Cross a cattle grid and immediately leave the lane to head for a waymarked stile on the left. Cross and follow a clear route descending towards the lower right had corner of the field. Skirt to the left of a brick building and pass through a gate in the far right hand corner of the field. Follow a short path between hedges to reach a second gate and steps onto a road.

4 Turn LEFT and follow the road to the junction opposite the Knighton Hotel, signposted for Clun and the Railway Station. Turn RIGHT and follow the road past the

the waymarked gate on the left and continue AHEAD to a waymarked post by the River Teme. Turn LEFT, go through gate, cross railway line with care and go over footbridge to the right. Turn LEFT, descend steps and go through gate onto riverside path. Follow this through three kissing gates into wood. Continue to follow path until just past the riverside picnic area. Take the path on the right, leading up to the grassy area behind the Offa's Dyke Heritage Centre. Follow the clear path left across the grass, go up the steps and head RIGHT along the gravel path to reach the Centre.

3

WALK 2

GARTH HILL

DESCRIPTION This easy 3¼ mile walk starts from Offa's Dyke Heritage Centre and takes a short cut to join Glyndŵr's Way on the edge of Knighton, from where there are excellent views over the town. From here, the route follows the long distance trail through woodland that allows further views across the valley to the course of Offa's Dyke Path on the Shropshire Hills. After a section of walking along a quiet lane, the route leaves Glyndŵr's Way and joins a footpath running across fields on the south-western side of Garth Hill, allowing further attractive views across a valley. Once back in Knighton, Glyndŵr's Way is rejoined, to explore a quiet back lane and path in Knighton, before returning to the footpath shortcut back down towards the Heritage Centre. Allow about 2 hours for the walk.

START Offa's Dyke Heritage Centre, Knighton, SO 285725.

1 From outside Offa's Dyke Heritage Centre, go RIGHT. At the road junction, go LEFT on Heol Offa (signposted for Llandrindod Wells). At the top of the hill bear RIGHT. Continue AHEAD past the entrance to Radnor Drive, on the right. After a few yards, look out for a footpath sign set back to the right. Turn RIGHT and follow the path between hedges to the road. Go RIGHT across a small car park and turn LEFT to go up the steps to the right of the houses. Follow the path to the right and then to the left, going up steps to a stile. Cross and head HALF RIGHT up the field, with the path gradually becoming clearer, to reach a further stile onto Glyndŵr's Way.

2 Cross and turn RIGHT on Glyndŵr's Way. After a few yards, take the right fork and descend slightly, with railings to the right. Follow Glyndŵr's Way through the woods, passing two waymark posts and three stiles. Ignore a footpath leading off to the right and continue AHEAD on Glyndŵr's Way, which soon runs between hedges. Pass two more waymark posts on the right to reach a further waymark post at the junction with a lane. Go LEFT on the lane. Bear LEFT at the first junction and RIGHT at the second. Follow the lane down, past a bench on the right, to the turning for Little Cwmgilla.

3 Continue AHEAD on the lane, leaving Glyndŵr's Way. Before reaching the second exit from Little Cwmgilla, follow the path up the bank to a waymarked stile on the left. Cross and follow a path AHEAD up through the trees and to the left of the fence. At a waymark post, continue AHEAD (skirting the damp area at this point). Follow the path along the bottom of the hill, to the right of a hedge. At a fork in the path, take the right fork. Continue AHEAD between hill and fence. Ignore the first stile and continue AHEAD to cross a second stile near a farm building. Go HALF RIGHT past metal railings and cross a track to a waymarked stile.

4 Continue to the right of the field, then head for a waymark post to the left of a barn. Go past the barn and a second waymark post on the left. Follow the track, taking the right fork after a few yards. Towards the end of the field (now in sight of Knighton) bear HALF RIGHT to reach a stile to the right of a gate. Cross and follow the right boundary of the field to reach a stile onto a lane. Turn RIGHT on lane and go round bend to the left. Shortly afterwards, follow Glyndŵr's Way HALF LEFT past houses and along a track.

5 On reaching a Glyndŵr's Way waymark post (where the long distance trail was joined on the outward journey), cross the stile on the right and head HALF RIGHT down the field to another stile. Cross and follow the path down to the estate houses. Go RIGHT across the small car park and bear LEFT down to the path between hedges. At the road, turn LEFT. Continue past the entrance to Radnor Drive and at the next junction, follow the main route downhill to the left. At the next junction, go RIGHT to return to the Offa's Dyke Centre, on the left.

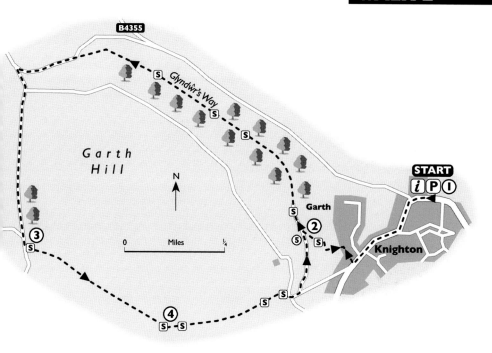

Garth Hill

WALK 3

FRYDD WOOD & OFFA'S DYKE

DESCRIPTION This moderate 4¼ mile walk heads south from Knighton, following Offa's Dyke Path up through Frydd Wood and along the edge of a local golf course to reach hill country with a range of excellent views. The walk passes through a number of organic upland meadows, with clover, buttercups, celandine and a range of other flowers. Sections of Offa's Dyke can be seen alongside the route, first to the right and then to the left. In the later stages the route follows a quiet lane and footpath back to Knighton, joining Glyndŵr's Way for an additional walk around some of the attractive hidden areas of Knighton before returning to the Heritage Centre via the street known as The Narrows (the start of Glyndŵr's Way) running down to the Knighton Clock Tower. Allow about 3 hours for the walk.

START Offa's Dyke Heritage Centre, SO 285725.

1 From outside Offa's Dyke Heritage Centre, go LEFT. Go past the Clock Tower and down Broad Street. At the Knighton Hotel, on the right, go RIGHT through the archway to the car park. Cross the car park and continue AHEAD on Larkey Lane. Go uphill, past the bench on the left. At the junction with main road, cross with care. Head a short distance to the RIGHT and then follow Offa's Dyke Path sign to the LEFT. Head between the houses. Turn RIGHT just before the garages. At the far end of the garages, go HALF LEFT on a waymarked path.

2 Follow the path uphill. Cross a lane and go up the steps. Continue on Offa's Dyke Path up through Frydd Wood. Cross a stile and go RIGHT keeping to the left of a fence (the golf course can be seen off to the left along this stretch of the route). Keep to the right of the next four fields, connected by waymarked stiles. In the fifth field, follow the right hand boundary and then cross Offa's Dyke near an Offa's Dyke Plinth. Cross a stile on the right and turn LEFT. Follow the left hand boundary of the next two fields, connected by stiles, with Offa's Dyke visible on the left.

3 Cross the middle of the next field to a stile. Continue AHEAD to a further stile. Go along the right hand side of the next two fields, connected by stiles, to a lane. Turn RIGHT on the lane. Go RIGHT at the next junction, passing houses on the right. Go past a farm on the left. Go past the first stile, on the right, and cross the second stile, also on the right. Go along the left hand side of the field and through a waymarked gate. Continue along the left hand side of the next field to reach a gate in a dip in the far left hand corner.

4 Turn RIGHT on the lane. Go past Seamus Ryan Construction, on the left. Descend the hill to Upper Woodhouse Farm. Continue down the lane to the junction with the A4113. Cross the main road with care and go AHEAD on Penybont Road. Go past a bench and a bus stop on the right. After a few more feet, turn RIGHT on Glyndŵr's Way. Follow the path between hedges and cross a driveway. Follow the path down and to the left, passing a cottage. Go LEFT along the lane for a short way.

5 Take the right fork and follow the lane and then path AHEAD. Pass to the right of Weaver's Cottage. Head along the lane and, when this bears right, head HALF LEFT up a path. Cross a lane and continue up the path ahead. Follow Castle Road AHEAD and then round to the LEFT. After a few yards, turn RIGHT into a pedestrianised lane (The Narrows). Head down towards the Town Clock. At the junction, turn LEFT to return to Offa's Dyke Heritage Centre.

6

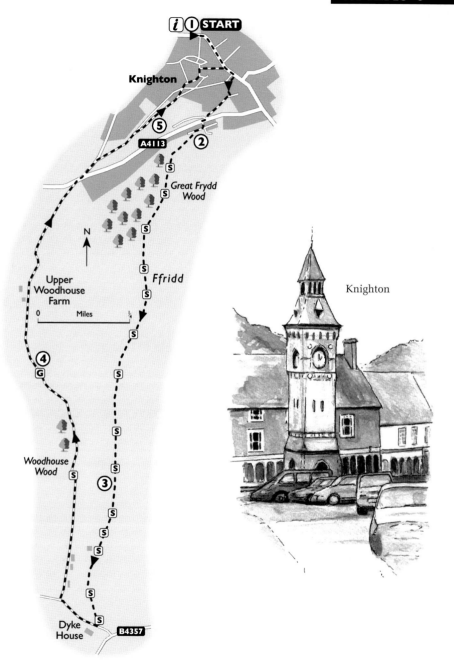

START

Knighton

⑤

A4113

②

Ⓢ

Ⓢ Great Frydd
Wood

Ⓢ

Ⓢ

Ⓢ

N

Upper
Woodhouse
Farm

0   Miles

Ⓢ Ffridd

Ⓢ

Ⓢ

Ⓢ

④
Ⓖ

Ⓢ

Ⓢ

Woodhouse
Wood   Ⓢ

③

Ⓢ

Ⓢ

Ⓢ

Ⓢ

Dyke   Ⓢ
House   B4357

Knighton

7

KINSLEY WOOD

DESCRIPTION A moderate 3¾ mile walk that goes along riverside and past St Edward's Church to enter Kinsley Wood. This Forestry Commission woodland is in the process of being transformed from conifers to a mixture of oak and other broadleaved trees. The route taken gives good views over the valley to the east and passes a pool and site of oak tree plantings. After passing a viewpoint looking down onto Knighton, the walk descends, partly through mature oaks and exits the wood to join Offa's Dyke Path. Continuing down hill, the route crosses a lane to reach the Teme, following a scenic and level riverside route to a picnic area near the Offa's Dyke Heritage Centre. Allow some 2½ hours for the walk.
START Offa's Dyke Heritage Centre, SO 285725.

1 From outside Offa's Dyke Heritage Centre, follow the driveway round to the back of the centre. Follow the gravel path, passing benches to the left, to reach a way-mark post below trees. Go down the steps on the right, pass the first waymark post and head cross the grass to a second post near the trees. Follow the path down to the right and turn RIGHT on the riverside path. Go through a gate and across a small car park. Take the left fork in the road ahead. Follow the road round to the right and then to the left. At the road junction, go RIGHT and almost immediately LEFT. Pass St Edward's Church. At the next junction, continue AHEAD down to the main road.

2 Go LEFT and follow main road over the railway bridge. Turn RIGHT and continue to the end of the pavement. Cross main road with care and take the waymarked path opposite. Follow the path up through the woods. At a junction of tracks, go LEFT and LEFT again on a vehicle access route. Follow this broad track, *which gives excellent views of the valley to the east.* Continue uphill and take the left fork in the track. At a parking area (by information board) go SHARP LEFT past a vehicle access barrier.

3 Follow the track past a bench on the right and take the next turn to the RIGHT. Pass to the right of a pond, near which oak planting has been carried out. Continue AHEAD on the main track until this veers to the right. At this point, take the left fork and descend to join a broad track at the viewpoint over Knighton. Turn RIGHT and follow the track past a bench on the right. Continue AHEAD and, when the main track bends right and begins to climb, take a path leading down HALF LEFT.

4 Continue along the path, descending steeply at one point, to cross a stile out of the wood. Continue AHEAD to an Offa's Dyke Path waymark post. Turn LEFT and descend the hill to a gate onto a lane. Cross, go through a second gate and continue AHEAD to a waymark post by the riverbank. Turn LEFT and follow the riverbank to a gate. Cross the railway line WITH CARE and head RIGHT over the footbridge. Turn LEFT through another gate and follow the riverside path.

5 Go through a kissing gate onto a gravelled path. Follow this through two more kissing gates. Continue AHEAD into riverside woodland, passing an old bridge on the right. Just beyond the riverside picnic bench, turn RIGHT and go up path by wooden railings. At the top, turn LEFT and head across grass to a waymark post. Go up steps and turn RIGHT. Follow the gravel path to return to the Offa's Dyke Heritage Centre.

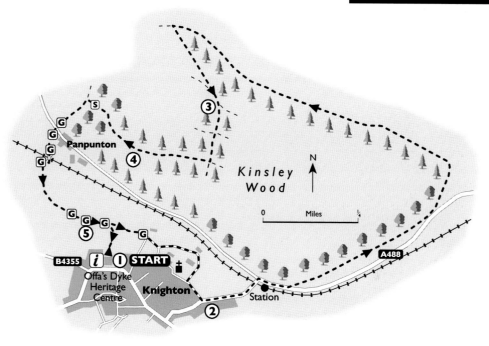

Kinsley Wood

N

0 Miles ¼

Kinsley Wood

9

PANPWNTON & CWM-SANAHAN HILLS

DESCRIPTION This moderate 7 mile walk starts by following Offa's Dyke Path along the River Teme and then up beside Kinsley Wood to the top of Panpwnton Hill. From here, the long distance trail follows the ridge of hills running along the English side of the Teme valley, affording great views towards Wales. The 13-arch railway viaduct at Knucklas can be seen across the valley. After passing the trig point on Cwm-Sanahan hill, the route descends (steeply in places) to Brynorgan. Here the route leaves Offa's Dyke Path, to follow a bridleway past the cottage and round to the other side of Cwm-Sanahan hill (the bridleway in the later stages is waymarked by Shropshire Countryside Services Team) affording views to the east. Rejoining Offa's Dyke Path between the two hills, the route retraces its outward course for a while, then descends to Bryney to join a waymarked footpath running along the base of the hills (providing an opportunity to look up at the summits walked along earlier) then joins a lane near Nether Skyborry. Finally, the route rejoins Offa's Dyke Path for a walk back alongside the Teme into Knighton. Allow about 4½ hours for the walk.

START Offa's Dyke Heritage Centre, Knighton, SO 285725.

I From outside Offa's Dyke Heritage Centre, go round to the back of the building. Follow the gravel path to the right of the benches to reach a waymark post below trees. Go down the steps on the right to a waymark post. Bear LEFT across the grass to a further waymark post. Bear RIGHT and go down the path to the riverside path. Turn LEFT and follow the path past an old footbridge and through a kissing gate onto a gravelled track. Continue AHEAD through two more kissing gates and follow the path along the side of the Teme. Go through a gate and go RIGHT over the footbridge. Cross the railway line

WITH CARE and go through a second gate. Follow the path along the river bank to a waymark post, then turn RIGHT and cross the field to a gate onto a lane.

2 Cross the lane and go through the way-marked gate opposite. Follow one of the paths uphill (these join once beyond the wood). Continue up the hill (*great views of the valley behind you*). Near the brow of the hill, take a left fork in the path. Go up the bank and bear HALF RIGHT to a waymark post near a field boundary. Cross a track and follow the path up to the left of a wood. At the end of the wood, continue AHEAD on a clear path through gorse. Go through a gate and continue AHEAD to a memorial to Roy Waites, *Chairman of the Offa's Dyke Society, 1970-80*. Continue AHEAD, following the path to the left of the fence and passing through three gates.

3 Pass to the right of barns, go through a further gate and cross a track. Follow the path along the left hand side of a wood and bear RIGHT above a valley, crossing a stile and eventually another track. Still keeping to the left of the fence, follow the path past two waymark posts. Continue up to a third waymark post and, after a few yards, reach trig point on Cwm-Sanahan hill (*the highest point on the route*). Keeping still to the left of the fence, cross two stiles and then follow three waymark posts on the path down to Brynorgan. Go through the gate on the right, into the cottage garden, and exit by a gate on the far side. Follow the track to a junction of tracks just before a gate onto a lane.

4 Turn RIGHT and follow the other track round to the other side of Cwm-Sanahan hill. Pass through a waymarked gate. Head along the left hand side of four fields, connected by waymarked gates and with a clear track for most of the way. On nearing an old barn, off to the left, take the right fork in the route, near a waymark post on the left. Follow the track down to a gate, pass through and turn LEFT on Offa's Dyke Path. Keeping to the right of a fence, cross a stile and follow the path along above a the valley, past the wood and round to the left.

Follow Offa's Dyke Path back to the next track. Turn RIGHT here and follow the track down to Bryney. Go LEFT at the cottage and leave the track to follow a waymarked footpath leading off HALF RIGHT.

5 Pass through a short belt of trees and descend to the left of a laid hedge. Follow a path through the bracken, cross a footbridge and stile. Head RIGHT for a few feet, then continue AHEAD to the left of a fence (the path becomes clearer as it descends). On reaching a gate on the right, bear LEFT. Follow the path to the left of the fence. At a waymark sign, head HALF LEFT up to a further waymark post. Continue to the left of the fence to reach a waymarked gateway. Continue AHEAD, still to the left of the fence. At the next waymark (on fence), descend to and cross a small stream.

6 Cross a stile under the trees ahead. Continue AHEAD to the left of the fence and then head LEFT to a stile. Follow the path down for a few yards to reach a track. Head LEFT on this. Cross a stile and continue for a few yards to a tarmac lane. Take the right fork down to a lane. Turn LEFT and follow the lane to the point where this is crossed by Offa's Dyke Path, just before Panpwnton Farm. Turn RIGHT through a gate and continue AHEAD to a waymark post by the river. Head LEFT to retrace the riverside route back to the Offa's Dyke Heritage Centre.

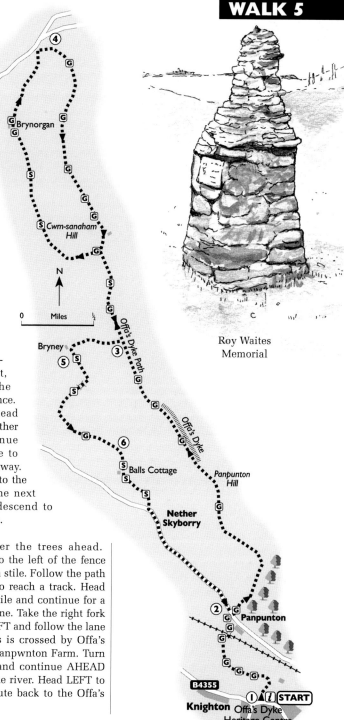

Roy Waites Memorial

11

WALK 6

LLANWEN HILL, THE SPACEGUARD CENTRE AND CWM IFOR

DESCRIPTION A moderate 7½ mile walk from Offa's Dyke Heritage Centre, through Knighton and then by bridleway, lane and footpath to the Spaceguard Centre on Llanwen Hill with its excellent views over the surrounding countryside. After an opportunity to visit the Spaceguard Centre (see www.spaceguarduk.com for details) the route returns down the lane and retraces the footpath to Farrington Lane, from where an attractive bridleway is followed to Mount Farm. Here the walk joins a footpath running along the attractively wooded Cwm Ifor, alongside the Pont-Faen Brook for most of its route, before heading back down into Knighton. (NB The east-west track shown on OS maps of Llanwen Hill has no legal status as right of way or unclassfied road and is not therefore used as part of this route). Allow 4¾ hours, plus about 1½ hours to tour the Spaceguard Centre.

START Offa's Dyke Heritage Centre, Knighton, SO 285725

1 From outside the Heritage Centre, turn LEFT and follow the road past the Town Clock. Descend Broad Street, passing the turning for the railway station. Continue AHEAD on the Ludlow Road, passing Harry Tuffins (on the left) and the Presteigne Road (on the right). Continue just past the school and take the next turn to the right. Follow the road round to the left, ignoring side turnings. When the road bends to the right, head HALF LEFT and join a waymarked bridleway on the right. Follow this up between hedges to reach a lane.

2 Go right along the lane, passing Farrington Farm, on the right. At the end of the tarmac section, take the waymarked track on the left. Head down and through the farmyard at Llanwen Farm, exiting by a gate on the far side. Follow the left hand side of the field to a stile. Cross and continue along the left hand side of the next field. Go through the right hand gate and follow the left hand side of another field to reach a gap (which may contain low sheep hurdles). Go through the gap (or cross hurdles) and go along the left hand side of a third field to a gate. Pass through and continue AHEAD along the access track to reach the junction with a lane

3 Turn RIGHT and follow the lane uphill for about one mile, then turn RIGHT on a track signposted for the Spaceguard Centre. After visiting the Centre, return along the access track, turn LEFT and descend hill to the turning for Farrington. Retrace the outward route along the access track, past Farrington and along the right hand side of the three fields to Llanwen. Go back through the farmyard and up the track to Farrington Lane. Turn LEFT and follow the track for a few yards to the bridleway sign on the right.

4 Turn RIGHT through the gate. Follow the right hand side of four fields, connected by waymarked gates. Continue along the right hand side of the fifth field. Just before the end of the field, turn RIGHT through a waymarked gate. After a few yards, go LEFT through another waymarked gate. Turn RIGHT and follow the right hand side of the field to a gate. Cross a narrow field to a further gate. Head RIGHT along and then down the bank to the access drive to The Mount Farm. On nearing the road, bear RIGHT across the grass to a gate some yards to the right of the drive entrance.

5 Turn RIGHT on the road and, after a short distance, take the waymarked footpath on the right. Cross the stile and descend 7 steps. Bear LEFT across a grassy clearing and continue AHEAD between rock outcroppings and Pont-Faen Brook. Cross a second and third small clearings in the wooded valley. At a fork in the path, take the right fork. Cross a fourth small clearing and go through a gap in an old fence line. Head along the

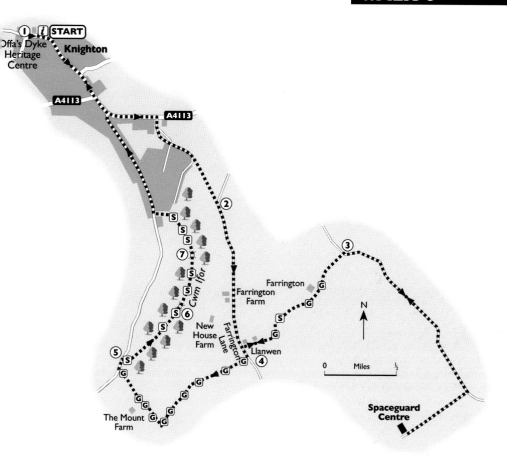

lower, right hand, edge of the field and cross
a stile next to an old gate. Continue half way
along the right hand side of the next field,
then cross a footbridge and stile on the right.

6 Turn LEFT and follow the left hand side
of the field to a stile at far end. Follow
the old track AHEAD. Look out for a path
crossing the track, just beyond a fallen tree
off to the left. Turn LEFT here and follow the
path down the bank towards the stream (there
is currently no waymarking at the junction,
but a few yards down the path there is a yellow waymark arrow on a tree to the left). At
the bottom of the bank, head RIGHT, skirting
fallen trees to reach a stile. Follow the path
AHEAD for a few yards, then cross the footbridge on the left.

7 Go up a short bank and turn RIGHT.
Follow the path along the lower edge of
the field, using a well trodden route to skirt to
the left of a fallen tree. Continue on the main
path, to the left of Pont-Faen Brook. On nearing a house, head LEFT up the bank to a stile.
Continue AHEAD on a path to the left of the
fence. Cross a stile and head up a small field
to another stile. Follow the path AHEAD to
join a road. Turn RIGHT and follow the road
(the Presteigne Road) down to the junction.
Turn LEFT and follow the main road back into
Knighton. Go up Broad Street and pass the
Town Clock to return to the Heritage Centre.

CALECK'S POOL & STOWE

DESCRIPTION An easy walk of about 6 miles, following a mainly riverside and footpath route to Caleck's Pool, before joining enclosed green lanes and other footpaths. The route then leads down to cross the main road and follow a lane over the Teme and join a footpath leading up to the village of Stowe. A further footpath crosses a ridge, providing views ahead to Kinsley Wood and Knighton. The route then crosses further fields to pass through Kinsley Wood and follow a riverside path back to the Offa's Dyke Heritage Centre. Allow about 3¾ hours for the walk.

START Offa's Dyke Heritage Centre, Knighton SO 285725.

1 From outside Offa's Dyke Heritage Centre, turn LEFT. Follow the road towards the centre of town. On reaching the Town Clock, turn LEFT and follow the road down to St Edward's Church. Turn RIGHT just before the church and follow the road down to the junction with the main road. Cross with care and head LEFT towards the railway station. Just before reaching the first entrance to the station area, turn RIGHT and follow a lane and then a path to a gate. Go through and follow a well-used path HALF RIGHT across the field to another gate. Turn LEFT and follow the path. At the junction of paths, turn RIGHT and continue AHEAD to join a road in a trading estate. Follow the road round to the left and right to reach the main road.

2 Cross the main road and take a minor road slightly to the left. Follow the road up to a waymarked gate on the left, just below Llanshay Farm. Go through gate and across the field to a further gate. Follow the boundary fence of Llanshay Farm, which leads round to the right to reach a waymarked gate into the farmyard. Go through the gate and turn LEFT to pass through another waymarked gate. Follow the track along the left hand side of the field to a further gate, just beyond which is Caleck's Pool. Go past the pool, following the track at first, then head up to the far right corner of the field. Go through the left hand of two waymarked gates. Follow the remains of an old track along the left hand side of the field to a gate.

3 Go through the gate and head LEFT on an enclosed green lane. Follow the green lane round to the left, right and then left again. Look out for a waymarked stile on the right. Cross this and head RIGHT across the brow of the hill and follow the right hand side of the field to a waymarked stile. DO NOT CROSS THIS, but turn LEFT and cross a number of cart tracks. Continue AHEAD between fences and go through a waymarked gate on the right. Head HALF LEFT down the field and then down the bank to a waymark post. Turn LEFT and follow the old hedgeline to a gate into the wood.

4 Follow the track through the wood to a stile. Cross and head along the right hand side of the large field to a stile in the far right hand corner. Cross and cross the main road with care. Head RIGHT along the verge to the turning on the left towards Stowe. Follow this turning over the Teme, over the railway line and to the crossroads. Turn RIGHT, signposted for Weston and Cubbage. Follow the lane which at first runs close to the railway line. After about half a mile, when lane bends left away from the railway line, look out for a stile set back on the left. (This can be found just before the hedgeline thins out). Cross the stile and head along the right hand side of the first field. At the far side, go through the waymarked left hand gate and along the right hand side of the field. Before reaching the farm, go through a waymarked gate on the right and turn LEFT. Follow the left hand side of the field to a stile on the left. Cross and go down the steps. Turn RIGHT and follow the track to the lane.

START

Offa's Dyke Heritage Centre

Knighton

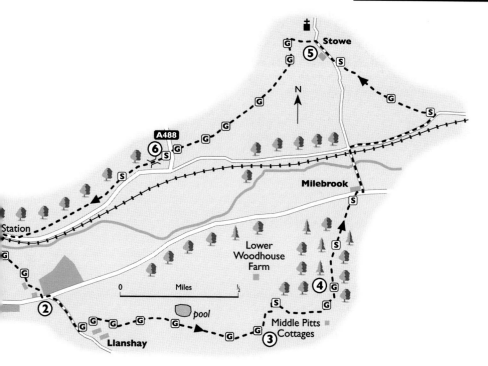

5 Turn RIGHT and follow the lane round to the left. When the lane bends to the RIGHT, by the Old Vicarage on the left, turn LEFT on a track. Just before the cattle grid, go up the bank on the left and through a gate. Go up the right hand side of the field, ignoring a small gate on the right. Cross a track and go through the waymarked gate ahead. Go down the left hand side of the field. Go through the gate with care (broken hinges at present) and continue along the left hand side of the next two fields via waymarked gates. Go along the right hand side of the final field to a gate and descend bank to main road – TAKE CARE HERE. Cross main road and head LEFT to a stile.

6 Cross and head over the field, crossing a footbridge to reach a stile below trees near the top left corner of the field. Cross and go up the steps. Turn RIGHT and follow the vehicle access track uphill for a short way, then turn LEFT on another track. In a few yards, go RIGHT at a junction of tracks. Continue AHEAD until reaching the road near the railway station. Cross road with care and follow pavement right and over railway bridge to the left. Follow the main road to the T-junction near the Knighton Hotel. Turn RIGHT and follow Broad Street uphill. Go past Town Clock to return to the Heritage Centre.

CALECK'S POOL & LLANSHAY DINGLE

DESCRIPTION An easy walk of around 4 miles, passing through the centre of Knighton and crossing a riverside field before heading up to follow footpaths, lanes and green lanes past four attractive local pools and then follow a bridleway back into Knighton. Allow about 2½ hours for the walk.

START Offa's Dyke Heritage Centre, Knighton, SO 285725.

1 From outside Offa's Dyke Heritage Centre, turn LEFT. Follow the road towards the centre of town. On reaching the Town Clock, turn LEFT and follow the road down to St Edward's Church. Turn RIGHT just before the church and follow the road down to the junction with the main road. Cross with care and head LEFT towards the railway station. Just before reaching the first entrance to the station area, turn RIGHT and follow a lane and then a path to a gate. Go through and follow a well-used path HALF RIGHT across the field to another gate. Turn LEFT and follow the path. At the junction of paths, turn RIGHT and continue AHEAD to join a road in a trading estate. Follow the road round to the left and right to to reach the main road.

2 Cross the main road and take a minor road slightly to the left. Follow the road up to a waymarked gate on the left, just below Llanshay Farm. Go through gate and across the field to a further gate. Follow the boundary fence of Llanshay Farm, which leads round to the right to reach a way-marked gate into the farmyard. Go through the gate and turn LEFT to pass through another waymarked gate. Follow the track along the left hand side of the field to a further gate, just beyond which is Caleck's Pool. Go past the pool, following the track at first, then head up to the far right corner of the field. Go through the right hand of two way-marked gates.

3 Follow the enclosed track ahead to a further gate. Continue AHEAD along the right hand side of the field, passing an old gateway. Follow the waymarked track round to the right, with an enclosed pool to the right. Continue on the track, which now bends left (*excellent views over Knighton from here*). Go through a large red gate and head HALF RIGHT to a second large red gate. Follow the track to the left to reach a waymark post beyond two trees. Cross the track and head up the field, to the left of the house, making for a waymark post at the top of the field. Cross a stile onto a minor road.

4 Turn RIGHT and follow the road down hill. This route gives good views over Knighton and clearly shows the transformation work in progress in Kinsley Wood. On reaching Llanshay Farm (on the right) turn SHARP LEFT into Farrington Lane. Cross Llanshay Dingle, where a further two pools can be seen, to either side of the lane. Pass the bungalow on the left and follow the lane up a small hill. When the lane bends to the left, turn RIGHT on the enclosed bridleway, by a waymark post. Folllow this down to a road. Follow the road AHEAD, ignoring side turnings, to reach the main road near the school. Turn LEFT and follow the main road back into Knighton. Go up Broad Street, past the Town Clock to return to the Heritage Centre.

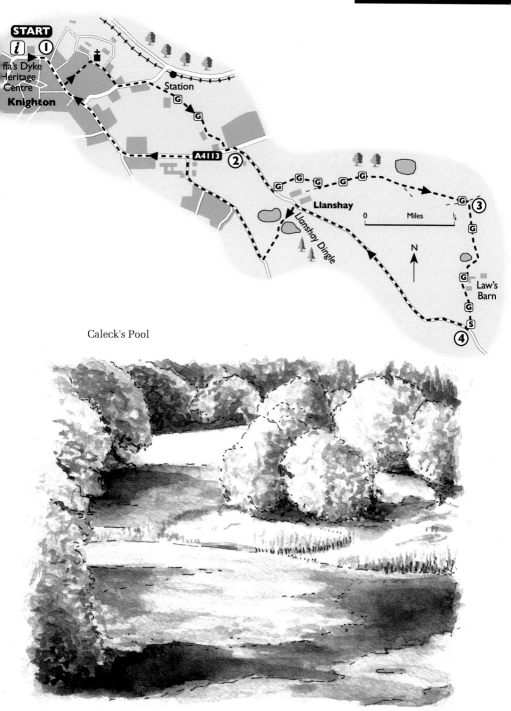

Caleck's Pool

WALK 9

COED DETTON

DESCRIPTION This easy 4¾ mile route leads through the edge of Kinsley Wood and via footpath and road to Coed Detton, a traditional oak woodland containing a circular track and footpath route passing through a beautiful range of woodland scenery and allowing a view of the scenic hills above Stowe. Allow about 2¾ hours for the walk. **THIS ROUTE INCLUDES ABOUT ⅓ MILE ON AN A-ROAD, ON WHICH CARE IS NEEDED.**
START Offa's Dyke Heritage Centre, Knighton, SO 285725.

I From outside Offa's Dyke Heritage Centre, follow the driveway round to the back of the centre. Follow the gravel path, passing benches to the left, to reach a waymark post below trees. Go down the steps on the right, pass the first waymark post and head cross the grass to a second post near the trees. Follow the path down to the right and turn RIGHT on the riverside path. Go through a gate and across a small car park. Take the left fork in the road ahead. Follow the road round to the right and then to the left. At the road junction, go RIGHT and almost immediately LEFT. Pass St Edward's Church. At the next junction, continue AHEAD down to the main road.

2 Go LEFT and follow main road over the railway bridge. Turn RIGHT and continue to the end of the pavement. Cross the main road with care and take the waymarked footpath opposite. Follow the track up through the woods. At a junction of tracks, go RIGHT and then LEFT on a vehicle access route. After a few yards, when the vehicle access

track bends sharply to the left, go RIGHT and descend a flight of steps to a stile. Cross and head for a stile on the far side of the field, crossing a footbridge on route.

3 Cross the stile and head LEFT along the main road TAKING CARE ON THIS SECTION OF THE ROUTE. After about half a mile, on reaching a footpath sign on the right, bear RIGHT on a track that leads through a gate into Coed Detton. Follow the track for about ¼ mile to a junction of tracks. Turn RIGHT and follow the track up a short hill and then along through the wood. On reaching the gate at the end of the wood, turn back – there is no right of way across the field to join the footpath coming up from Stowe.

4 On the way back, look out for a path leading off half left – this will be reached before reaching the short hill section of the track. Turn LEFT onto the path and follow this down to the junction with the track used to enter Coed Detton. Turn LEFT and follow the track back down to the road. Turn LEFT along the main road TAKING CARE ON THIS SECTION OF THE ROUTE. Pass the farm and house on the right and continue to reach the stile on the right.

5 Cross and head over the field, crossing the footbridge to reach the stile by the trees. Cross the stile and go up the steps to the vehicle access route. Follow this to the right and soon turn LEFT on another track. Follow this through the edge of Kinsley Wood to re-enter Knighton near the Railway Station. Cross the railway bridge and follow the road into town, going RIGHT at the T-junction near the Knighton Hotel. Head up Broad Street and continue AHEAD on reaching the Town Clock, to return to Offa's Dyke Heritage Centre.

18

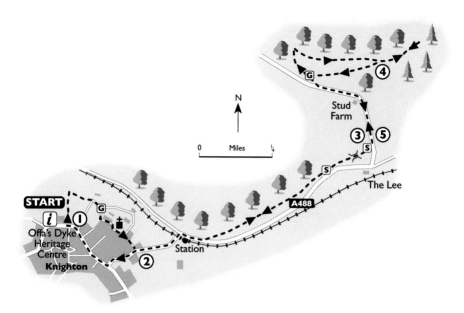

Knighton

CAER CARADOC

DESCRIPTION This strenuous 11 mile walk starts from Knighton and follows Offa's Dyke Path along the River Teme before taking a short cut to reach the line of the Dyke above the Teme valley. After following Offa's Dyke Path along the hill for a way, the route turns east and follows an old track across the hill to Five Turnings. Via an attractive lane and then foot-path route above the Redlake valley, the walk leads the open access land area that includes the prehistoric fort of Caer Caradoc. A walk around the hill fort, which will be additional to the main 11 miles, provides an excellent oppor-tunity to see a wide range of views. From here, the route follows footpath and track to join a BOAT (byway open to all traffic) running along the hills above Stowe, before taking a footpath route down to near Stowe and returning to Knighton via fields and Kinsley Wood. Allow 7 hours for the walk, in addition to time spent at Caer Caradoc.

START Offa's Dyke Heritage Centre, Knighton, SO 285 725.

I From outside Offa's Dyke Heritage Centre, go round to the back of the build-ing. Head across the grass to the right of the benches to reach a waymark post below trees. Go down the steps on the right to a waymark post. Bear LEFT across the grass to a further waymark post. Bear RIGHT and go down the path to the riverside path. Turn LEFT and follow the path past an old foot-bridge and through a kissing gate onto an enclosed track. Continue AHEAD through two more kissing gates and follow the path along the side of the Teme. Go through a gate and go RIGHT over the footbridge. Cross the railway line WITH CARE and go through a second gate. Follow the path along the river bank to a waymark post, then turn RIGHT and cross the field to a gate onto a lane.

2 Cross the lane and go through the way-marked gate opposite. Follow one of the paths uphill (these join once beyond the wood). Shortly after leaving the wood, bear HALF LEFT on a path through the bracken

(before reaching the first waymark post). Follow the path through alternate patches of bracken and clearer ground, pass through a small group of trees, followed by old gate-way (care – remains of gate on ground in gap) and continue in the same direction. On reaching clearer ground, cross a track and continue AHEAD to the right of gorse bushes. Continue to gradually ascend the hill, skirting a large patch of thistles and join Offa's Dyke Path near a waymarked gate.

3 Go through the gate and follow Offa's Dyke Path along the hill, keeping to the left of the fence. Pass through two way-marked gates, follow the long distance trail to the right of hill top barns and go through another waymarked gate onto a track. Turn RIGHT on the track and go through a waymarked gate. Follow an old trackway between trees on left and fence on right. Pass through a further waymarked gate into a large field. Follow the track along the right hand side of the field. On reaching a waymark sign on the right, head HALF LEFT to the far left corner of the field. Go past two waymark posts to reach a further gate. Follow the old track along the right hand side of the field to reach a gate onto the A-road.

4 Cross with care and take the lane opposite, to the right of Five Turnings Cottage. Continue past 'Peugot Breakers', *soon with good views over the Redlake val-ley to the left*. Continue past Garn Farm (on the left) and Wax Hall (on the right). Before the lane bends to the left, go through a way-marked gate on the right. Bear HALF LEFT across the field to a gate part way up the field. Follow the left hand side of four fields, connected by gates. Begin to descend the hill, passing a waymark post on right, near gorse bushes. Look for and cross a stile bear-ing 'Access Land' symbol, on the right.

5 Climb gradually up to the summit of Caer Caradoc – following the boundary of the hill fort gives a wide range of excellent views. When ready, return down hill to the footpath – Chapel Lawn hamlet, in the valley, makes a good visual reference point. Turn RIGHT and follow the path down through bracken to a stile below trees. Cross and

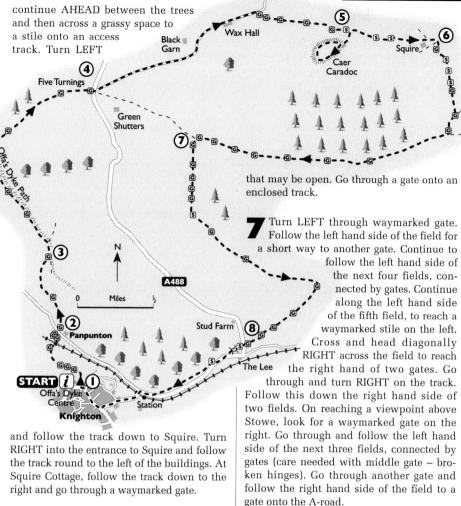

continue AHEAD between the trees and then across a grassy space to a stile onto an access track. Turn LEFT

that may be open. Go through a gate onto an enclosed track.

7 Turn LEFT through waymarked gate. Follow the left hand side of the field for a short way to another gate. Continue to follow the left hand side of the next four fields, connected by gates. Continue along the left hand side of the fifth field, to reach a waymarked stile on the left. Cross and head diagonally RIGHT across the field to reach the right hand of two gates. Go through and turn RIGHT on the track. Follow this down the right hand side of two fields. On reaching a viewpoint above Stowe, look for a waymarked gate on the right. Go through and follow the left hand side of the next three fields, connected by gates (care needed with middle gate – broken hinges). Go through another gate and follow the right hand side of the field to a gate onto the A-road.

and follow the track down to Squire. Turn RIGHT into the entrance to Squire and follow the track round to the left of the buildings. At Squire Cottage, follow the track down to the right and go through a waymarked gate.

6 Go AHEAD on the track. Ignore the first stile and follow the track to the left. Pass two waymark signs and follow the old track up the right hand side of the field to a stile. Continue up the right hand side of two fields, crossing a stile. At top of the second field, cross a stile and turn RIGHT. Go through a gate and follow the track to the right of the field to a further gate. Continue along the right hand side of the next field to meet a track. Turn RIGHT and go through a waymarked gate. Follow the track along the hill, passing a forestry entrance on the right. Continue to follow the track along the right hand side of five fields, connected by gates

8 Cross the A-road with care and go over the stile opposite. Cross the footbridge and head up to a stile below trees, near the left hand corner of the field. Cross and go up steps to a vehicle access track. Go RIGHT and shortly LEFT. Follow the track round to the right and through Kinsley Wood to rejoin the A-road near the railway station. Cross with care and follow pavement over the railway bridge and into town. At the T-junction near the Knighton Hotel, turn RIGHT. Go up Broad Street, passing the Town Clock to return to the Offa's Dyke Heritage Centre.

21

RAGGED KINGDOM & HOLLOWAY ROCKS

DESCRIPTION A moderate walk of about 8¼ miles, via woods and fields to the attractive village of Stowe. From here a route is followed through Ragged Kingdom mixed wood and across fields with a range of hill views to a high point near forestry on Stowe Hill. The return route leads down past the picturesque Holloway Rocks and returns to Stowe. A quiet lane route and then footpath via Kinsley Woods are followed on the rest of the return to Knighton. Allow about 5 hours for the walk.

START Offa's Dyke Heritage Centre, Knighton, SO 285725.

I From outside the Offa's Dyke Centre, turn LEFT and follow the road past the Town Clock and downhill to the turning for the railway station. Turn LEFT here and follow the road past the Horse and Jockey public house and over the railway bridge. Go RIGHT and follow the pavement to its end. Cross the main road with care and take the footpath leading into Kinsley Wood. Follow this uphill and then along through the wood. At a junction of tracks, take the right fork. On reaching a vehicle access track, go LEFT. After a few yards, when the access track bends sharply to the left, go RIGHT down a flight of steps and over a stile. Head across the field to a second stile on the far side, crossing a footbridge on the way.

2 Cross the stile and cross the main road with care to reach a gate in the hedge, slightly to the left. Follow the left hand side of the field to a gate. Go through and follow the right hand side of the next two fields, connected by gate (care needed – broken hinges at present). Continue up the right hand side of the next field to reach a way-marked gate at the further end of the field.

Go through and cross the track. Follow the fence on the left down hill ignoring a small gate in the fence. At the lower end of the field, go through a gate and descend the bank to join a track (to the right of the cattle grid). Turn RIGHT and follow the track to the junction with a lane.

3 Turn LEFT and follow the lane up to Stowe Church. Continue on the track. bearing LEFT and follow the track through the woods to reach a gate. Go through and turn SHARP LEFT. Follow a track that climbs steeply for a while and then heads round to the left. Go through a gate and continue straight AHEAD to reach a gate into Ragged Kingdom woods. Follow the track through the woods to reach a gate at the further end. Follow the left hand side of the field to another gate. Continue along the left hand side of the second field to the far left corner.

4 Turn RIGHT and follow the track for a few yards, then bear HALF RIGHT on a path that leads diagonally up the field and then to the right. Go through the gate and follow the track AHEAD across the next field. Go through the gate and head SLIGHTLY LEFT across field **START** *i* ① to pass through a narrow belt of trees to a stile. Cross and continue HALF LEFT towards the planta-tion ahead. On reaching a track, turn RIGHT and follow this until reaching a footpath exiting the plantation.

Offa's Dyke Centre

Knighton

5 Turn RIGHT and follow the footpath across the hill and down the track past Holloway Rocks to reach a gate. Go through and follow the track down past a pond on the right to reach a further gate. Go through and follow the track back towards the left to reach the lane near Stowe Church. Continue down the lane until this bends sharply to the left. Turn RIGHT onto a track. Just before a cattlegrid go up the bank to a gate on the left. Go up the right-hand side of the field

22

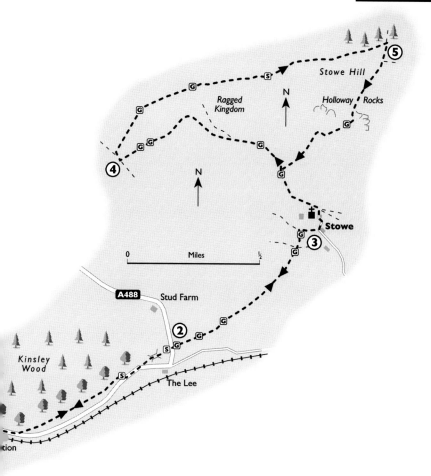

(ignoring a small gate on the right). Cross a track and go through a waymarked gate. Follow the left-hand side of three fields, connected by gates (take care – there are broken hinges on the middle gate). Go through a gate and along the right-hand side of the field to a gate onto an A road. Cross with care to reach a stile on the far side. Cross and head over the footbridge and up the field to stile below trees near the left hand corner of the field. Go LEFT on vehicle access track, then take turning to right. Follow this back to Knighton, going back over railway bridge and into town. At the T-junction, turn RIGHT and retrace route past the Town Clock to reach Offa's Dyke Heritage Centre.

WALK 12

TO KNUCKLAS

DESCRIPTION This easy 4 mile walk follows a short stretch of the River Teme, before heading up to cross Glyndŵr's Way and follow a footpath route up to a lane on the top of Garth hill (with great views back towards Knighton). The quiet lane is then followed, to once again cross Glyndŵr's Way and follow a lane up to open access land (the site of a former racecourse). The walk follows a track along the open access land and then takes to a footpath that crosses organic hill fields before descending on the lane to Knucklas (with views of Knucklas railway viaduct and Knucklas castle site on route). Passing under the viaduct, the walk ends at the local (request) railway station for transport back to Knighton. Allow ablout 2½ hours for the walk.

START Offa's Dyke Heritage Centre, SO 285725.

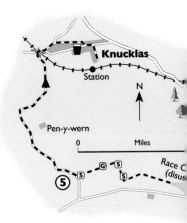

From outside Offa's Dyke Heritage Centre, go round to the back of the building. Follow the gravel path to the right of the benches to reach a waymark post near the trees. Turn LEFT (heading away from the steps on the right) and follow the path to an Offa's Dyke plaque. Take the path to the left of the plaque, with wooden railings on the right. Turn RIGHT and follow the path to the right of a hedge to reach a large Offa's Dyke plinth. Bear RIGHT to folllow the path across Offa's Dyke and cross the grass to the nearer waymark post below trees. Go down the path and turn LEFT. Go through the first kissing gate and continue most of the way along the path to the next kissing gate.

2 Just before the gate, turn LEFT and head for the far left corner of the field. Go through a kissing gate and cross the road with care. Go LEFT on the pavement. At the road junction, turn RIGHT. Follow the road uphill and bear RIGHT at the junction. Follow the road past the entrance to Radnor Drive, on the right. Look out for a waymark post set back to the right. Turn RIGHT and follow the path between hedges. Bear RIGHT across a small car park and turn LEFT to fol-low a path up past houses. Follow the path RIGHT and then LEFT to cross a stile into a field.

3 Folllow the path HALF RIGHT up the field to a stile onto Glyndŵr's Way. Turn RIGHT and follow Glyndŵr's Way for a few feet, then bear LEFT on a waymarked footpath. Go up the bank and continue uphill following a path through bracken and then across a buttercup-rich field – *with good views back towards Knighton.* Pass to the right of a waymark post near a hedge on the left. Follow the path up a bank and across a stile onto a lane. Turn RIGHT and follow the lane (passing the turning for the hill top mast) to reach a T-junction.

4 Turn RIGHT and shortly afterwards turn LEFT at the next junction, signposted for Llangunllo 4 miles. Follow the lane up past Rhos y Garth. Cross the cattlegrid and bear RIGHT on the open access land. Follow the track to the left of the hedge and then fence, now on the site of the old racecourse. Towards the end of the open access land, cross a stile on the right. Cross the left hand side of the field to a further stile. Turn LEFT and follow the left hand side of the field to a gate. Continue along the left hand side of a further field to a stile onto a lane.

5 Turn RIGHT and follow the lane down to Knucklas, with views of the viaduct and castle hill on the way. At the T-junction, turn RIGHT to pass under the viaduct. Take the

24

left fork and follow the road through the village to pass the The Castle pub, on the right. Take the side road leading off to the right to reach Knucklas Station (request stop – signal as for a bus) to return to Knighton.

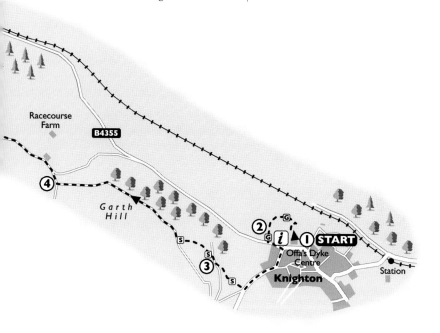

Castle Inn
Knucklas

WALK 13
KNUCKLAS VALLEY WALK

DESCRIPTION Starting from Knucklas Railway Station, from which there are excellent views across to the Shropshire Hills, this easy 2¾ mile walk passes under the 13 arch railway viaduct at Knucklas. To the right can be seen Knucklas Castle, site of a prehistoric hill fort and said to be the place where King Arthur and Queen Guinevere married. The route follows a footpath route across fields, then joins a bridleway to pass through a stretch of woodland and across open fields, with a beautiful valley view off to the left. Joining an unfenced lane, also the route of a bridleway, the walk heads back down the valley to return – again by passing under the impressive viaduct – to Knucklas Station. Allow some 2 hours for the walk.

START Knucklas Railway Station or roadside parking nearby, Knucklas, SO 254741.

I Follow the exit route from Knucklas Station and continue down the road ahead to the T-junction (if arriving by car, join the route near the T-junction). Turn LEFT and follow the road running to the right of the Castle Inn public house.

Continue AHEAD past a bridge on the right, beyond which can be seen Knucklas Castle hill. Go under the Railway Viaduct.

2 Ignore the first lane leading off to the left and the second lane, which is also marked by a bridleway sign. Continue along the road for some yards further, looking out for a footpath sign on the left. Turn LEFT here and cross the stile into the field. Head HALF RIGHT to reach a second stile in the far right corner of the field. Cross and follow the left boundary of the field to a further stile. Cross and continue ahead towards the buildings at Pentrusco. Cross a stile to the left of a gate.

3 After a few yards, turn SHARP LEFT and follow the bridleway up through the wood, ignoring turnings off to the right. Exit the wood via a gate and continue AHEAD across the field to a gateway. Continue AHEAD across a further five open fields, on a track that soon becomes easier to see. The views on this section are well worth a pause or two. On reaching an unfenced lane near Cwm Jenkin, turn LEFT onto the lane.

4 Follow the lane down past Lower Dolwilkin and alongside the picturesque

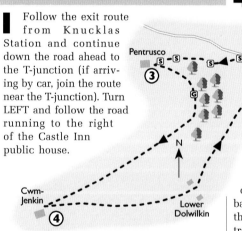

King's Brook to reach the junction with the road followed earlier. Turn RIGHT and follow the road back under the viaduct. Take the left fork and follow the road back past the pub and to the right turning for the railway station. If you are catching the train, please note that Knucklas is a request stop and the train should be signalled as for a bus.

26

WALK 14

AROUND BUCKNELL

DESCRIPTION An easy walk of some 4½ miles around the pleasant Shropshire village of Bucknell, with its range of half-timbered and other interesting buildings. The walk also includes an exploration of the scenic Redlake valley. Allow some 2¾ hours for the walk.

START Bucknell Railway Station, SO 356 737.

1 Leave the railway station and head LEFT over the level crossing, with care. Turn RIGHT, signposted for Hopton Heath, and follow the road round to the left and past the Sitwell Arms public house. Turn LEFT on the path that leads past the picturesque Old School House and continue AHEAD to the right of the church. Turn RIGHT on reaching the road opposite the village Post Office/shop/cafe.

2 On reaching the junction near the phone box, with large tree in middle of grassy area, follow Dog Kennel Lane AHEAD. When the lane bends to the right, take the bridleway on the left. Follow the path up beside a stream and through a gate into the field. Go up the right hand side of the field to a gate. Follow an old track and then continue along the left hand side of the next field to a gate onto a lane.

3 Turn LEFT and follow the no-through lane past Willow Cottage, on the right. Look out for, and join, an enclosed green track on the left. When the green lane becomes a track, follow this to a gate into a field. Continue along the left hand side of three fields, connected by gates. Continue AHEAD passing through two gates by Hillside Cottage. Follow the tarmac lane down to the point where this bends sharply to the left towards a gate.

4 Turn RIGHT at the bend in the lane and follow the track to a gate into the wood. Take the left hand fork in the track and follow this through a mixture of woodland and bracken covered hillside to reach a gate into forestry. Go through the gate and follow the path AHEAD and to the LEFT to join a forestry track. Go LEFT on this and pass through a gate (care needed – no hinges at present). Continue along the track to reach a gate onto a lane.

5 Turn LEFT and follow the lane over the Redlake and back towards Bucknell. After about one mile, on the edge of Bucknell, head LEFT down the no-through road near the ford. Cross the footbridge and head RIGHT along the lane, with the River Redlake to the right. At the junction, cross the road, turn LEFT and follow the course of the Redlake (note Baron of Beef public house across the road). On returning to the junction near the phone box, turn RIGHT and cross the bridge. Turn LEFT at the church and follow the path round to the lychgate. Bear round to the RIGHT and follow the lane back to the road.

6 Turn LEFT and follow the road for a few yards, then bear RIGHT on the path that runs past the school. Turn LEFT and follow pavement back to the turning for the railway station. NB Some trains only stop at Bucknell by request – signal the driver as for a bus.

27

OFFA'S DYKE PATH & JACK MYTTON WAY 1

DESCRIPTION This moderate 5½ mile walk starts from Lloyney in the picturesque Teme Valley, on the border between Wales and England. It then follows the Jack Mytton Way (Shropshire's 100 mile long cycling, horseriding and walking route) up a wooded lane and past the farm at Graig. Shortly after, the Jack Mytton Way joins a track running between hedges and then up towards the open hills, to meet Offa's Dyke Path near Llanfair Hill. The two long distance routes run together for some way, down a hill with some spectacular views and with some of the best preserved stretches of Offa's Dyke close by. On reaching Garbett Farm, minor lanes are followed towards Graig Farm, where the route rejoins the Jack Mytton Way and descends back to Lloyney. Allow 3½ hours for the walk.

START Lloyney, Teme Valley north-west of Knighton, SO 245 758

1 Cross the bridge near Lloyney into Shropshire, following the Jack Mytton Waymark signs. At the T-junction turn right. Take the first turning to the left, signposted (on the right) for the Jack Mytton Way. Follow the lane up past houses on the right and through the wood to reach the large farm at Graig. Folllow the lane round to the left and go straight AHEAD on a narrow lane between hedges and farm buildings. When the lane bends sharply to the right (after about ¼ mile) take the track running straight ahead.

2 Pass through a gate and continue AHEAD on the track. At first this runs mainly between hedges but, as it climbs steadily towards the hills, the views open out over Shropshire and back towards Wales. On reaching the farm buildings at Llandinshop, pass through a gate and turn RIGHT. Go past the buildings and through a second gate. Take the right fork in the track, passing through a third gate. Ignore the signs for a bridleway that crosses the track and continue AHEAD on the enclosed track, with a range of excellent views available on the route. In due course go through another waymarked gate (the line of Offa's Dyke is now indicated by a row of trees off to the right).

3 Go through the gap in the line of Offa's Dyke and pass through a waymarked gate. Turn RIGHT and follow a grassy track to another waymarked gate. Pass through and go HALF RIGHT down the hill, with Offa's Dyke to the right and further hill views towards Wales. Follow the clear track down towards Garbett Hall, going through one waymarked gate across the track and at the end of the next field, bearing to the right to reach a second waymarked gate. Continue to follow the track down hill, now with Offa's Dyke to the left. Pass through one more gate to reach Garbett Hall.

4 Just before reaching the main house, bear LEFT and go through a gate onto a lane. Turn RIGHT and follow the lane down for about ½ mile to Selley's Cross. Turn RIGHT on a narrow lane that leads uphill and then makes a long descent to pass the turning for Upper Treherbert. Follow the lane uphill once more to meet the course of the Jack Mytton Way. Turn LEFT and follow the narrow lane back to Graig Farm. Go RIGHT through the farm and follow the lane back down through the wood. At the junction, go RIGHT and soon cross the bridge on the left to return to Lloyney.

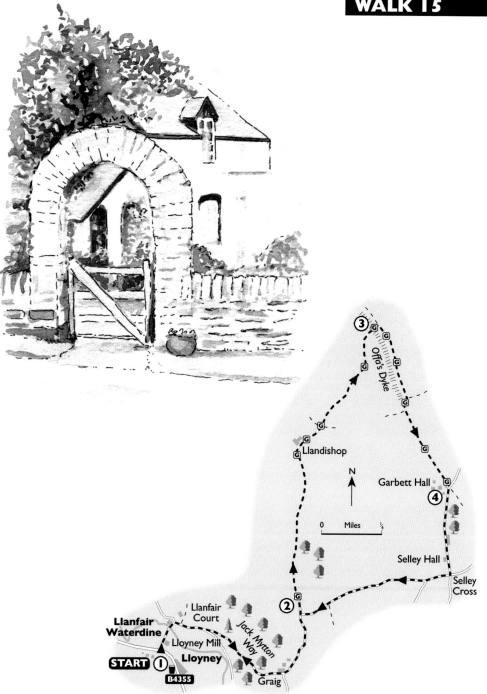

OFFA'S DYKE PATH & JACK MYTTON WAY 2

DESCRIPTION This moderate 5½ mile walk starts from a roadside location between the picturesque valleys of the Teme and the Clun. It follows the course of two long distance trails, Offa's Dyke Path and the Jack Mytton Way across the hill tops, affording a range of excellent views and with some of the best pre-served sections of Offa's Dyke visible nearby. On reaching the descent towards Garbett Hall, the route leaves Offa's Dyke Path to follow a bridleway with Shropshire Countryside Services waymarkings across the hill and down via Cwm Burholes to a minor road. The road, flanked by trees and woods, is followed for about ¾ mile to reach a bridleway passing Brook House and crossing fields, with views over the surrounding countryside, to rejoin the course of Jack Mytton Way. Passing through a section of Offa's Dyke and following an uphill section of lane leads back to the roadside parking area. Allow 3½ hours for the walk.

START Roadside between Teme and Clun valleys, SO 249796 (limited parking on the verge – two or three cars only).

I From the roadside, follow the track to a three-way fingerpost. Turn RIGHT, fol-lowing the course of both the Jack Mytton Way and Offa's Dyke Path. Follow the track, which affords excellent hill views to the right. Pass through two waymarked gateways (gates may well be open). Offa's Dyke gradu-ally approaches the track from the left. Pass through a third gate (which again may be open) and a fourth (which may be closed).

2 When the track bears left through the Dyke, leave the track and cross the stile on the right. Follow the path along the top of the Dyke itself – this is a grassy section that passes to the right of woodland and sheep sheds (the course of Offa's Dyke Path can sometimes be used as sheep holding areas at this point). Cross the next stile and continue along the course of the Dyke. At the third stile, when Jack Mytton Way passes through the Dyke, go LEFT on the track. Go through a waymarked gate and take the grassy track leading to the right and through another gate.

3 Follow the track HALF RIGHT, with Offa's Dyke visible on the right and some excellent hill views ahead. Descend the hill, passing through a waymarked gate on the way. Towards the end of the next field, when Offa's Dyke Path heads towards a gate on the right, turn LEFT and follow a track along the right hand side of the field. Go through a waymarked gate. Continue along the right hand side of the second field, then bear SLIGHTLY LEFT to a waymarked gate. Go across the third field to a waymarked gate. Bear LEFT for a few feet, then follow the fence line on right. At the far end of this long field, cross a waymarked stile to the left of a gate.

4 Follow the grassy track AHEAD, with a view of the valley opening up as you go. On reaching another track, turn LEFT (by a fallen waymark post on left). Follow the track down towards Cwm Burholes (note the tree planting off to the right). Keep to the left of the fence and, at the bottom of the field, turn RIGHT and follow the track along to and across a small stream. Go through a gate, along a short section of track and through another gate onto a lane. Turn LEFT and fol-low the lane along a wooded valley, passing Upper Treverward and Barnacre (both on the right). Cross the bridge and follow the lane up to the turning for Brook House, on the left.

5 Follow the bridleway down the drive, passing the pond and go through a gate to the right of the house. Follow a short waymarked path between gorse bushes AHEAD. Continue uphill, to the right of a small stream. Bear RIGHT to reach the brow of the hill, then head LEFT along the long field to reach a waymarked gate above a dingle on the right. Follow the high ground AHEAD and then the fence on the right to reach a waymarked gate. Follow the right hand side of the field to join the Jack Mytton Way (which comes through a gate on the

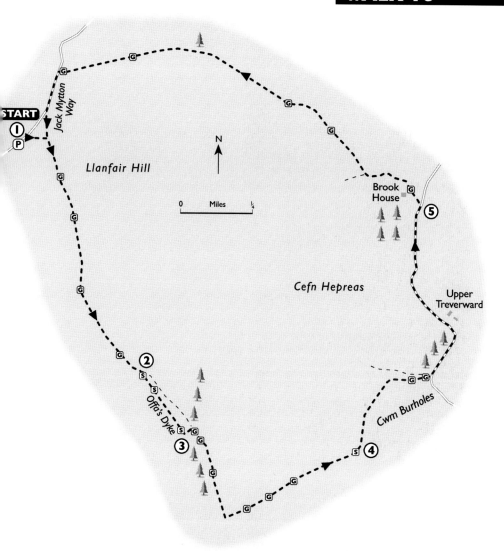

right). Continue along the track to the next waymarked gate. Pass through a gap in Offa's Dyke and continue along the track to a gate onto the road. Turn LEFT and follow the road uphill back to the roadside parking area.

WALK 17

KNUCKLAS TO KNIGHTON

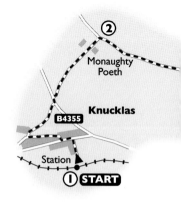

DESCRIPTION This moderate 4 mile walk soon leaves Wales for the south Shropshire Hills, by way of a quiet lane route to Skyborry Green. From here the walk climbs steadily, with the view providing plenty of reasons to pause and look back into Wales, to the house at Bryney. Entering what is now open access land, the walk follows a track past rock outcroppings and near hill top barns to join Offa's Dyke Path on route to Knighton. From the latter stages of the walk, there are very good views down on the serpentine course of the Teme and onto Knighton. The walk ends with a riverside section of Offa's Dyke Path. Allow 2½ hours for the walk.

START Knucklas Railway Station, SO 254741.

1 Follow the exit route from Knucklas Railway Station. Go down the road ahead. At the junction, turn LEFT. At the pub, take the right fork. Before reaching the railway viaduct, turn RIGHT over the bridge and RIGHT again. Follow the lane to the junction with the B-road. Cross with care and take the lane just to the left, leading towards Monaughty Poeth. Cross the Teme into Shropshire and at the junction, turn RIGHT, signposted for Skyborry Green ¾ and for Knighton.

2 Follow this quiet lane for ¾ mile (views to the hills on the left along which Offa's Dyke and Offa's Dyke Path run). At Skyborrry Green, turn LEFT and immediately head HALF RIGHT on a track (signed with 'Vehicle Access to houses only'). Follow this past the farm buildings and through two gates (which may be open). Continue AHEAD up the steep track to reach Bryney. Go through the waymarked gate just to the left of the house.

3 Continue uphill for a few yards to reach two waymark posts. Follow the course indicated by the left hand post, following a track up and to the right. Go through a gate and bear RIGHT on the track. On reaching rock outcroppings, on the left, follow the track round to the left. Go through a second gate and follow the track to the right. On reaching open hillside bear HALF LEFT on the track (hilltop barns visible to the left) to reach the course of Offa/'s Dyke Path, with the Dyke itself just beyond.

4 Turn RIGHT and follow Offa's Dyke Path along the left hand side of four fields, connected by waymarked gates. Pass the hilltop memorial to Roy Waites, Chairman of the Offa's Dyke Society, 1970-80. Continue through a further gate and follow the path AHEAD past gorse bushes and down hill to the right of the trees. Before reaching the three-way waymark post, bear HALF RIGHT on a path running downhill. Bear RIGHT at the next junction of paths and descend the clear route through the bracken and on down hill to reach a gate onto a lane.

5 Cross the lane and go through a second gate. Continue AHEAD to a waymark post by the riverbank. Turn LEFT and follow Offa's Dyke Path through a gate, across the railway line (with care) and RIGHT over a footbridge. Go LEFT through a gate and follow the riverside path to a kissing gate. Follow the gravelled path through a further two kissing gates and along a path through woodland, passing a 'Welcome to Wales' sign by an old bridge. Pass the riverside picnic area and bear RIGHT, with railings on the right. At the top of the bank, turn LEFT and follow the clear path across the grass

32

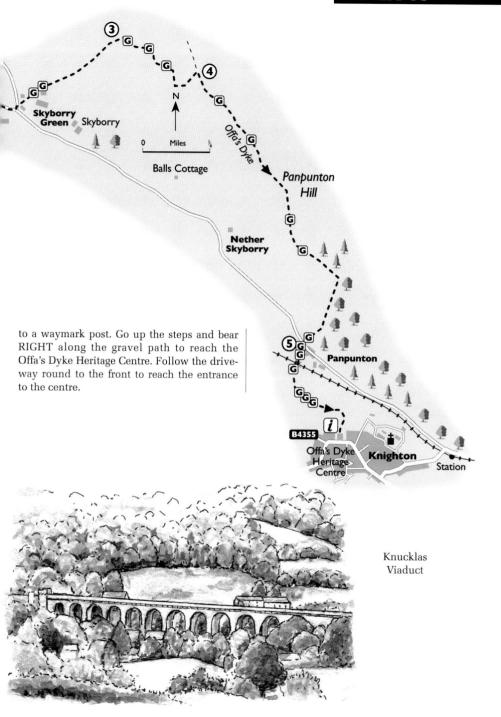

to a waymark post. Go up the steps and bear RIGHT along the gravel path to reach the Offa's Dyke Heritage Centre. Follow the driveway round to the front to reach the entrance to the centre.

Knucklas Viaduct

GLYNDŴR'S WAY & HILL VIEWS

DESCRIPTION This moderate 7½ mile walk starts from the site of an old racecourse (now open access land) and follows a lane that allows some great views across towards the Shropshire Hills, with Knucklas Castle (where King Arthur is said to have married Queen Guinevere) in the foreground. Joining Glyndŵr's Way, the walk leads across hills, now with views to the east and south, before passing the attractive holiday accommodation at Cefn-suran (farm trails also described alongside the route). Continuing along Glyndŵr's Way leads to a junction with a lane, which is followed back towards the old racecourse affording excellent views back over the outward route. Allow about 4¾ hours for the walk.
START Roadside parking at old racecourse/open access land, on minor road west of Knighton, SO 256732.

by trees on the skyline. Nearer to hand are the views of Knucklas Castle and Railway Viaduct. Continue past the footpath sign on the right. At the second footpath sign, on the left, turn LEFT through the gate (this is the original route of Glyndŵr's Way). Follow the track along the right hand side of the field to join the current route of Glyndŵr's Way.

2 On reaching the Glyndŵr's Way waymark post, go through the gate ahead. Follow a track along the left hand side of the field and cross a waymarked stile. Continue AHEAD past the sheep pens and go through a gate. Head along the left hand side of the field to a

I Continue west along the old racecourse. At the end of this continue AHEAD along the lane, passing an (unmarked) turning for Knucklas on the right. *The views on this stretch of lane include the south Shropshire Hills, with the line of Offa's Dyke indicated*

waymarked stile, then follow the left hand side of a long field to a waymarked gate. Follow the track along the left hand side of a further field – on reaching a pond on the left, follow the track half right to a waymarked gate. Pass the 'Country Code' notice, on the right, and follow an old track down between gorse bushes. Just before the 'No Entry' sign on the gate ahead, turn LEFT through a waymarked gate.

34

3 Descend the bank for a few yards, then bear RIGHT towards a waymark post. Head across the field to a second waymark post near a track. Bear LEFT on the track across the bridge. Turn HALF RIGHT and follow a clear track leading up and along the field. On coming to waymarking on a fence to the right, turn RIGHT and follow the signs downhill to a waymarked gate. Go through gate and head along the right hand side of

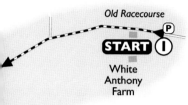

Old Racecourse

P

START (**1**)

White
Anthony
Farm

the field, to the right of the trees. Aim for the far right hand corner of the field to find a waymarked gate near the trees. Go RIGHT and shortly RIGHT again at a waymark post. Cross the grass to a waymark post by a cattlegrid. Cross this and bear LEFT on the track towards Cefn-Suran holiday accommodation. At the junction of

tracks, continue AHEAD (waymark post on right). Go through a gate to the right of a cattlegrid.

4 Approaching Cefn-suran, look out for the information board on the right, which describes the two farm trails. Just beyond this, leave the drive and go to the left of the playhouse to a waymark post below trees. Follow the path through the trees, over a stile and LEFT through a gate. Pass to the right of the barns, then turn RIGHT over a waymarked stile. Follow the track along the right hand side of the field, passing a large pond, to reach a waymarked stile. Follow the track through the trees and then head across the field to a stile to the right of the trees. Cut across the right hand corner of the field to reach a stile onto a lane.

5 Turn RIGHT on the lane. Follow this past Clogie, on the left, and Coed Harbour, on the right. Continue AHEAD, with extensive views to the right, over the area walked on the outward route. At the road junction, turn RIGHT and follow the hilltop route (*now with more views towards Knucklas and Shropshire*) back to the old racecourse.

WALK 19

TO BUCKNELL

DESCRIPTION A moderate 6 mile walk from Offa's Dyke Heritage Centre, via the edge of Kinsley Wood and across fields to visit the attractive village church at Stowe, crossing a ridge from where there are views ahead and back towards Knighton. From here, the route follows a footpath with views across the valley and then a quiet lane, before taking an unclassified road through forestry land to reach the attractive Shropshire Village of Bucknell. The walk ends at Bucknell Railway Station, from which a train can be caught back to Knighton. NB Some trains stop on request, signalled as for a bus. Allow 3¾ hours for the walk.
START Offa's Dyke Heritage Centre, Knighton, SO 285725.

2 Cross the main road with care and take the footpath opposite, leading up and then along through Kinsley Wood. At a fork in the track, take the right fork. On reaching a vehicle access track, turn LEFT. In a few yards, when the track bends sharply to the left, turn RIGHT and descend steps to the stile into the field. Head across the field, towards a stile on the far side (crossing a footbridge on the way). Cross the stile and cross the main road with care, aiming slightly to the left to go through a gap in the hedge to a gate. Follow the left hand side of the field until reaching a waymarked gate; Go through and follow the right hand side of the field to the next waymarked gate. Continue

along the right hand side of the third field to a further gate – care is needed here, the gate has broken hinges – and continue along the right hand side of a fourth field (ignoring the first gate on the right) to reach a waymarked gate at the far side.

3 Go through the gate and cross a track. Follow the fence on the left, continuing past a small gate to reach the lower edge of the field. Go through the right hand gate and descend the bank to join a track to the right of the cattle grid. Turn RIGHT and follow the track to the junction with a lane. If wishing, take a detour up the lane to the left to visit the attractive village church at Stowe, afterwards returning down the lane. Follow the lane down to the farm (where the lane bends to the right). Leave the lane here, going along a track to the left, passing between farm buildings. Before reaching the house, go up steps on the left and cross a waymarked stile. Turn RIGHT and follow the right hand

1 From outside the Offa's Dyke Heritage Centre, follow the drive round to the back of the building. Follow the gravel path past the benches to the waymark post below the trees. Descend the steps on the right and follow the clear path across to the waymark post by the trees. Go RIGHT down the path to the riverside. Turn RIGHT and follow the path along and through the gate onto the small car park. Cross the car park and take the left fork in the road. Follow this to the right, left, right and left again, passing St Edward's Church. At the next junction, continue AHEAD to the main road. Turn LEFT and follow the main road over the railway bridge. Turn RIGHT and follow the main road until reaching the end of the pavement.

36

edge of the field, passing a waymarked gate on the right. At the far end of the field, go through a waymarked gate and continue AHEAD, now along the left hand side of the field. Towards the end of the field, continue AHEAD between fences, cross a stile and descend the bank to a lane.

4 Turn LEFT and follow the lane for about 1½ miles, passing the turning to Weston (on the left). On reaching Cubbat/Cubbage Cottage, bear HALF LEFT on an unclassified road up into forestry land Continue AHEAD on this route (ignoring side turnings until reaching the junction with a tarmac lane). Follow the lane, going RIGHT at the junc-

tion. Continue past a lane coming from the left and turn RIGHT at the next T-junction. Continue AHEAD, passing the Post Office and the church. At the junction just beyond the church, continue AHEAD. Avoid narrow section of road by following the path past the school on the right. Follow the road round to the left. At the next junction, turn RIGHT to reach the railway station.

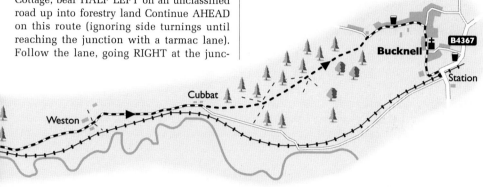

Bucknell
Station

BUCKNELL TO KNIGHTON

DESCRIPTION This moderate walk of 10½ miles passes through three counties – Shropshire, Herefordshire and Radnorshire. The Herefordshire Trail is followed for part of the route, from picturesque Brampton Bryan (church bell rung on the hour), through the attractive parkland setting around Brampton Bryan Park and Pedwardine Wood (crossing Heathy Park, an excellent area for views and blackberry gathering later in the year) to join a lane route along the side of a scenic valley. From here, the route follows a quiet lane uphill, with hill views to the right, then swings back towards Knighton. The next section includes lane, bridleway and footpath, with additional views, including of the Spaceguard Centre, before descending towards Knighton by a mixture of footpath and lane. Allow 6 hours for the walk.

START Bucknell Railway Station, SO 356737.

1 Leave Bucknell Railway Station and turn RIGHT on road signposted for Brampton Bryan, Knighton, Weston and Stowe. Continue AHEAD on the B4367 out of Bucknell (TAKE CARE – FAST TRAFFIC ON THIS ROAD). After about half a mile, turn LEFT on a minor road by white railings. Follow the minor road for about a mile. At the junction, turn RIGHT and follow the road across Parson's Pole Bridge (*now on the Herefordshire Trail*).

2 Follow the road past the walled grounds of the Castle on the right and the church to a crossroads in Brampton Bryan (like Bucknell, the church bell appears to be rung on the hour). Turn RIGHT here and follow the road past the village Post Office/shop. Leave the main road for a lane that passes to the left of attractive half-timbered cottages near a grass area (the lane is signed as 'Private Road/Parish Hall/Herefordshire Trail/Public Bridleway').

3 Follow the unfenced lane over two cattle grids, passing through attractive parkland. When the lane bends right, towards a third cattle grid, bear SLIGHTLY TO THE LEFT on a track across the grass (there is a marker stone on the left labelleded B/B.1 at this point). On reaching a white arrow, a stone to the left of the track, head uphill and follow the two waymark signs round to the left of the trees. Turn RIGHT and keep to the left of the trees, heading steeply uphill for a while and then following a path HALF LEFT to reach a gate into the wood (Herefordshire Trail marker on the far side of the gate).

4 Follow the path through the wood and across the open hillside at Heathy Park. On reaching a track, follow the white arrow waymarking to the left. On reaching animal pens, on the left, take the right fork in the track. Re-enter the woods and continue through these for some way.

Knighton

i

Offa's Dyke Heritage Centre

A488

Station

A4113

N

0 — Miles — ½

Law's Barn

⑧

Farrington Farm

Ⓖ Farrington

Ⓖ Ⓢ

Farrington Lane

Ⓖ

Ⓖ

Ⓖ

⑦

Ⓖ

Ⓖ

Ⓖ

Ⓖ

Ⓖ

Ⓖ Ⓖ Reeves Hill

⑥

Take the left fork at a junction, with a blue arrow waymark. After a few yards, take the right fork (look out for white arrow on a tree on left a short way down this track). On reaching a third junction, turn RIGHT and go through a gate out of the wood.

5 Follow an old track along the left hand side of the field to pass through a gate. Continue AHEAD on a track through the wood and then turn SHARP LEFT to reach a gate onto a lane. Turn RIGHT and follow the Herefordshire Trail along the scenic lane for about one mile. When the Herefordshire Trail branches off to the left, continue AHEAD on the lane to reach a junction. Turn RIGHT here and follow the lane up to Stonehill (*there are hill views to the right*).

6 At the next junction turn RIGHT again. After about half a mile, look out for a bridleway sign off to the right. Go through the gate on the right and immediately turn LEFT through another gate. Follow a path (rather faint at present) through the wood and exit via a gate. Cross a small field to the next gate and follow the fence line on the right. Pass another gate (with an electric fence set to sheep height to its left). Follow the electric fence on the right to reach a gate onto a lane, by a waymark post.

7 Turn LEFT and almost immediately go through a gate on the right (note yellow tape on one bar of the gate). Head along the field, parallel to the trees and then to the right of small hollows in the ground. At the far side of the field, pass through a band of trees and a gate. Continue AHEAD AND UP the next field, going gradually towards a gate (yellow tape) onto the road.

Turn RIGHT and follow the road in the direction of Knighton. Pass a bridlepath sign on the right and continue down the road.

8 After a short distance, turn LEFT on a way-marked track that leads towards Farrington.

Pass above the farm and go through a waymarked gate. Continue AHEAD along the right hand side of the field to two gateways. Go through the left hand gate-way (there may be sheep hurdles to cross here) and follow the right hand side of the field to another gate. Continue along the right hand side of the next field to a stile. Head up the right hand side of the field to a gate into Llanwen Farm yard. Go past the buildings and take the access lane leading up HALF LEFT to reach a lane. Turn right and follow the lane down past Farrington Farm.

9 When the lane bends to the right, bear HALF LEFT down a grassy track between hedges. On reaching a road go AHEAD to the junction, then head RIGHT and follow the road past the school to the main road. Turn LEFT and follow the main road back into Knighton.

Bucknell
START ①
Station
B4367
Lingen Bridge
A4113
Brampton Bryan ②
③
Brampton Bryan Park ④
The Herefordshire Trail
Heathy Park
Oak Hill
Pedwardine Wood
⑤
Boresford Farm
Hick's Farm
Willey Lodge

PRONUNCIATION

Welsh	English equivalent
c	always hard, as in cat
ch	as in the Scottish word loch
dd	as th in then
f	as f in of
ff	as ff in off
g	always hard as in got
ll	no real equivalent. It is like 'th' in then, but with an 'L' sound added to it, giving 'thlan' for the pronunciation of the Welsh 'Llan'.

In Welsh the accent usually falls on the last-but-one syllable of a word.

KEY TO THE MAPS

- Main road
- Minor road
- Walk route and direction
- ① Walk instruction
- - - - Path
- River/stream
- Ⓖ Gate
- Ⓢ Stile
- △ Summit
- Woods
- Pub
- Ⓟ Parking

THE COUNTRYSIDE CODE

- Be safe – plan ahead and follow any signs
- Leave gates and property as you find them
- Protect plants and animals, and take your litter home
- Keep dogs under close control
- Consider other people

Open Access
Some routes cross areas of land where walkers have the legal right of access under The CRoW Act 2000 introduced in May 2005. Access can be subject to restrictions and closure for land management or safety reasons for up to 28 days a year. Details from: www.naturalresourceswales.gov.uk. Please respect any notices.

Published by
Kittiwake Books Limited
3 Glantwymyn Village Workshops, Glantwymyn, Machynlleth, Montgomeryshire SY20 8LY

©Text & map research: Kittiwake Books Limited 2017
©Maps & illustrations: Kittiwake 2008
Drawings by Morag Perrott
Cover photos: *Main* – Knighton, inset – Knucklas Viaduct. David Perrott

Printed by Mixam, UK.

ISBN: **978 1 902302 60 7**